East of the Sun and West of the Moon

A Puppet-theatre Stage Play

Sigrid Undset

EVENTYR
BOOKS

East of the Sun and West of the Moon
by Sigrid Undset

Translation, introduction and notes by Simon Roy Hughes

This work is licensed under a Creative Commons Attribution 4.0 International License.

skriket@gmail.com

Cover illustration by Jenny Nyström (1854-1946)
Typeset in imfellEnglish using LaTeX.

Contents

Foreword	v
Dramatis Personæ	ix
Act i	1
Scene i	1
Scene ii	9
Scene iii	13
Act ii	15
Scene i	15
Scene ii	19
Scene iii	31
Act iii	35
Scene i	35
Scene ii	39
Scene iii	43
Act iv	47

Scene i	47
Scene ii	53
Scene iii	61
About the Author	67
About the Translator	69

Foreword

For Sigrid Undset, *East of the Sun and West of the Moon* was a labour of love, the culmination of a life-long interest in puppet theatre. Based on Asbjørnsen & Moe's folktale of the same name, Undset's play is not simply a retelling, but rather a reworking of the existing text, with details and motifs added by the Nobel laureate at the top of her game. This first English edition is published under a Creative Commons licence in the hope that someone somewhere will take the time and effort to stage *East of the Sun and West of the Moon* once again.

Puppet theatre was a regular feature of Sigrid Undset's life from the age of two; her grandfather hosted performances for the citizens of Kalundborg each summer. As she grew older, she entertained her younger sisters with her own puppet theatres, the stages of which were fashioned from matchboxes, which she glued together. She also produced the scenery and figures herself. The plays were of her own invention, though often adapted from the plots of novels she had been reading.

So it is hardly suprising that Undset's enthusiasm soared, when, in the mid 1920s, a neighbour invited her to inspect the puppet theatre he had made for his children. Eilif Moe was not only her neighbour, but also Sigrid Undset's lawyer, and their families were quite close. Enraptured, she promised on the spot to write a play for the theatre. The fulfillment of her promise may be read below.

By all accounts, Moe's puppet theatre was quite a grand affair. After procuring the services of Sigrid Undset, he enlisted the painter Alf Lundeby (1870-1961) to produce the puppets and set decorations, while Einar Fagstad (1899-1961) painted a 14m long scroll as a background. Reidar Brøgger (1886-1956) wrote a musical score. The play was first staged at the Moe's house, thereafter at Sigrid Undset's home. On both occasions, Undset voiced the troll hag, who appears in the last scene, complaining about the cook. After staging for Alf Lundeby's family and friends, *East of the Sun and West of the Moon* was performed in the children's ward of the hospital at Lillehammer.

Arguably the best-loved of the Norwegian folk narratives that are recognised around the world, "East of the Sun and West of the Moon" has been recorded from about 80 different

Norwegian raconteurs. Each telling brings in different motifs, and recounts the story in a slightly different way; Sigrid Undset's version of the tale is no different. One change she has made is the mixing of different variants. Although she has kept the social status of the farmer family, as per the eponymous tale, she has taken the name of the white bear from a variant, "White Bear King Valemon." The interest in the lives of the farmer family - their upward social mobility, the marriages of the other sisters, and so on - is wholly Undset's invention. Still, the occasion of Kari's wedding gives Mari a plausible motivation for wanting to see her family, which is often missing in the collected folktales.

Undset's play also moves away of the folktale genre by setting her plot firmly in space and time. Not only is the landscape and architecture characteristically Norwegian, but the troll hag in the fourth act names Hedal in Oppland as the location of the cook's previous engagement (p. 49), and before this the stage direction requires "city clothes from the 1820s" (p. 17). Undset's play is thus set in eastern Norway, some time in the 1820s. The setting ties in well with the conversation between Ola and the provost about the cultivation of potatoes, which is a plausible detail of the time and place. It seems the historical novellist of a playwright could not but indulge her passion.

East of the Sun and West of the Moon was first published

posthumously, on the occasion of Alf Lundeby's 90th birthday in 1960, replete with the vignettes and decorations Lundeby had produced for the publication in 1929 of Brøgger's musical score. It was republished in 1972. This is the first English edition, which has been released under a Creative Commons licence.

The reason for the Creative Commons licence is to make the play free for anyone to read, and lower any financial barrier to production. The licence allows adaptation - you are free to stage the play, or retranslate it into another genre or form. It also allows commercial derivatives, which, for example, allows theatres to charge for tickets, as a way of recouping investment, and (with any luck) turning a profit. If you do decide to do something with the play, please let me know. I am also willing to donate my time in an advisory rôle, if any matter needs further clarification. After all, this is a labour of love for me, too.

Simon Roy Hughes
Bodø, May 2020

Dramatis Personæ

White Bear King Valemon

Ola, a Tenant Farmer

Marte-Marja, his Wife

Guri ⎫
Kari ⎬ their Daughters
Mari ⎭

Their Small Children

The Provost

The Provost's Wife

Guests at Ola & Marte-Marje's Wedding

An Old Woman

An Even Older Woman

The Oldest Woman

The East Wind

The West Wind

The South Wind

The North Wind

The Moon

A Mound Fellow

A Mound Hag

A Hulder

The Troll Queen

Troll Daughter

Troll Maid

A Troll Hag

Three Small Princesses

Guests at the Troll Wedding

The Mountain Stricken

Act I

Scene 1 - 1

Outside a tenant farmer's cabin. Wood basket in foreground, stage left. Forest all the way up to the roundpole fence, stage right.[1] The tenant farmer stands on the bank, chopping wood.

MARTE-MARJE (*exiting cabin door*) Do you know where the girls are?

OLA I hear them down by the brook. I don't think they've finished the rinsing, yet.

MARTE-MARJE Huff! It's difficult when there's no peace in the evening, either. I don't like the girls being out so late; there's been such a noise around the house, the past few nights. (*Shouts*) Guri, Kari, Mari: Come up now!

REPLY (*off-stage*) Yes, mother.

---

[1] A roundpole fence consists of paired upright poles, with rough planking filling the space between them. The planking usually leans at an angle to the ground.

Enter the tenant farmer's three daughters from the background, stage right. They carry a bucket and a washingboard loaded with wrung-out clothes.

MARTE-MARJE Aren't you finished soon, father - so you can come in and eat?

OLA Yes, I'll be right there.

His wife and children go in.

OLA Well, it is a good thing I kept myself from telling the poor thing how things really stand; she would have been absolutely terrified. It's the strangest thing I've ever seen - he's trudged around and around the cabin. Outside the window, it looks almost as if he's stood staring in at us. - There was no sign of him, away by the barn. You might almost doubt it is a bear, even - although Bjørn-Ola is never mistaken when he sees bear tracks, especially upon wet ground.

WHITE BEAR comes roaring in from the right and pads forward towards the tenant farmer, who backs away.

OLA Dear Jesus!

He raises his axe.

WHITE BEAR No, no, you needn't be afraid. I come on a peaceful errand. Good evening, man.

OLA Well, you must excuse me; you were certainly a little unexpected. Good evening, White Bear.

WHITE BEAR Is it far to your neighbour's place, Ola?

OLA Yes, you and your kind are probably the closest neighbours that I know of. Where do you come from, then?

WHITE BEAR Oh, I live quite a way from here, though - farther than the farthest horizon you see away there.

The stars begin to twinkle forth.

WHITE BEAR You have three beautiful daughters, you do, Ola.

OLA Oh yes, they are good enough for me.

WHITE BEAR It'll be miserable for them to live by themselves, so far up in the forest.

OLA Perhaps it will.

WHITE BEAR I don't suppose you would have too much against marrying off one of them - if it were such that the son-in-law you gained could help you improve your lot a little, would you?

OLA (*sighs*) It's not even worth thinking about such things.

WHITE BEAR If you will give me one of your daughters, then I shall make you as rich as you now are poor.

OLA No, I most certainly will not. Things aren't so bad with us that I would sell my daughter off to a bear!

WHITE BEAR But you must not believe otherwise than that it shall go well with your daughter. She shall be treated as the finest queen.

OLA I shall have to talk about this with my wife first, of course - and then hear if the girl wants it.

WHITE BEAR That is reasonable. Perhaps you might ask them to come out for a moment, so that we can talk.

OLA I mean, I have to think about it a little first. You're not in any hurry, are you?

WHITE BEAR Well, it is so that I live a good distance away, so if it's all the same to you, then I would certainly like an answer right away. I have brought along a few things, too - nothing of any consequence - but if she doesn't despise it, then she shall use the like as my bride.

He reaches forth a great golden bridal crown.

OLA Hey, say there! That must weigh quite a bit - won't you come inside, then?

WHITE BEAR No, I'll wait over here by the fence, I will.

Goes over and sits on his haunches away by the path into the forest.

OLA (*goes up to the cabin door*) Oh, look out here a little, will you, Marte-Marja?

MARTE-MARJE (*in the door*) Yes, what is it? - Oh my, what is this? (*Shouts*) Inside with you, girls! Your gun, Ola - get hold of your gun!

OLA By no means, wife - this bear here, he is of a special kind, he is - he comes on peaceful errand, he says. He says he has come to propose to one of our daughters, he says.

MARTE-MARJE Oh what in the Lord's name shall we do now? Oh, hurry in after your gun, Ola! Inside with you, girls!

OLA No, wait a little. He sounds both decent and reliable. He says he will make us as rich as we now are poor, if he can have one of the girls.

GURI As rich as we now are poor? Then we shall be the richest farmer-folk both in this village and in the whole parish.

WHITE BEAR (*rises*) Your father shall be the richest farmer in the whole valley, girl.

GURI Huff, what a mess! Still, here we sit in the backwoods; we own nothing but the rags we stand and walk in. If I could be certain, White Bear, that you would keep your word, then ...

OLA (*whispers*) I think he has the means. For he gave me this and told me to give it to whomever should be his bride.

He shows her the bridal crown.

MARTE-MARJE Huff, but even so. I don't know how to say this, I don't, Ola - but I would much rather that the girl could find a husband who was of folk.

GURI Well, I don't know how that will happen; there hasn't exactly been a stream of suitors up here, that I know of. Don't weep, mother, I'm not afraid. Huff!

The WHITE BEAR *has risen and comes padding over.*

WHITE BEAR Is it you, then, who will dare to go with me and be my bride?

GURI (*swallows a couple of times*) Well, yes, I suppose I will.

WHITE BEAR Then you shall put on the crown, my bride, and bid your father and your mother farewell.

GURI (*puts on the crown. Shakes everybody by the hand in turn.*) Farewell, father, farewell mother - farewell everybody.

THE OTHERS Farewell, farewell!

MARTE-MARJE *weeps.*

WHITE BEAR Sit up on my back, and hold on firmly to my coat; we have far to go, and I must go quickly, for I must be beyond the farthest horizon before sunrise.

> Guri *sits up on the back of the bear. The others stand in a cluster at the corner of the cabin. The white bear moves off into the background.*

White Bear Here comes the moon. Do you see that mountain to the north, where it gleams like snow? Thither is where are headed, and even farther. Have you ever sat softer, have you ever seen so clear?

Guri (*falls to weeping*) On my mother's lap I sat softer. On my father's farm, I saw clearer.

White Bear (*cheerfully*) Well, then you're obviously not the right one.

> *Puts* Guri *down*

And so, well may you live!
(*Calls over his shoulder.*)
I shall return next Thursday evening; in the meantime, you must consider whether or not one of your other daughters dare try her luck.

> *The* White Bear *sweeps off into the forest. The tenant-folk enter,* Marte-Marje *at the rear, with her arms around* Guri, *who is weeping.*

Scene i - ii

Inside the tenant's cabin.

It is late evening, there is a storm outside, and the rain is beating on the windowpane. There is a fire in the fireplace, and its light shines out into the room.

Marte-Marje *stands by the fireplace, pressing the porridge,* Ola *sits on a stool close by, a little girl sits rocking a cradle, the smallest children play on the floor before.*

A long table along the window wall, in the background of the cabin. Guri, Kari *and* Mari *sit in a row on the bench beside the table.*

Mari is dressed in a black tunic, ready to travel, with a bridal crown on her head; she holds a small bouquet in her hand.

Marte-Marje No, I don't think he's coming in this weather. (Slowly.) I shouldn't be sorry for it, true to say.

Ola I do say, he has dealt fairly and squarely. He carried Kari home, and put her down on the threshold - when she lost her nerve. The girl suffered not even the least injury from the White Bear.

Kari No, he was both handsome and fine. - Even so, I grew afraid at last. He took me across both mountain and valley - and on and on we went. Finally, we came out on to a plateau high up in the mountains, and the bear ran with me so that the moss flew beneath his paws, and then we rode along the edge of some terribly high cliffs. And then he said that we should go down through the slopes. And, hold on tight now, he said, because it gets a little steep down here, and it's rather uneven - and then I lost my nerve, and he asked 'have you ever sat softer, have you ever seen clearer?' - and then I was no good for anything more, I wasn't, mother - I wished I was safe and sound at home again, and then I burst into tears, I did, and I said: 'On my mother's lap I sat softer; on my father's farm I saw clearer." 'Well then, you're not the right one,' said the White Bear King Valemon, and then he turned around.

Ola No, no, that's all very well. Nevertheless, I can't help but think that it would be pure good fortune, I think, for a poor tenant farmer's girl, if she could get such a husband as this white bear. He is rich, and he is kind too, and he is some kind of king, as far as I can understand …

Mari I can at least try; perhaps the bear will be satisfied with me!

MARTE-MARJE (*slowly*) Oh, I think I should be most happy if we had Mari home again - It's uncanny - and more - to have this bear trudging hither every Thursday evening.

MARI No, mother, don't say that. I am not afraid!

OLA Well, now you must be careful, Mari - so that the white bear doesn't bring you home, as he did both your sisters. You can understand, he must be something rather grand, he who is so careful about these things. - And he probably won't do too little for us, since we are to be the kin of such a luminary. You have to keep in mind, my child, that this concerns the welfare of all your siblings. -

MARTE-MARJE Oh huff, such weather we're having this evening; I can never believe he will come this evening -

GURI AND KARI Oh no, Mari, you'll never endure crossing the mountains on the back of the white bear on such a nasty night as this.

MARI I must try - don't weep so, mother. The White Bear hasn't done anything to my sisters, so I don't need to be afraid of him, either. You can be sure, father, that I shall remember what you have said, that this is for the welfare of you all.
(*There is a knock at the door.*)

WHITE BEAR (*outside*) Open up! Open up for White Bear King

Valemon.

(OLA *opens.*)

WHITE BEAR Are you ready to go with me, my bride?

MARTE-MARJE Oh no, oh no, are you out walking in this terrible weather, too?

WHITE BEAR Yes, it was raining and it was blowing as I made my way hither. Are you ready to go with me, my bride?

MARTE-MARJE You've come so late tonight, we thought you must have been prevented.

WHITE BEAR It has grown late and we have to arrive before sunrise; I cannot tarry. Are you ready to go with me, my bride?

MARI Yes, I am ready. Farewell, mother; farewell, father; farewell everyone.

Exit MARI *and* WHITE BEAR.

Scene I - III

Mountainous landscape.

A white morning moon hangs in a yellow-red sky of the approaching sunrise. In the background a steep rock wall with the likeness of a portal in the stone.

The White Bear *with* Mari *on his back, appears on the edge opposite the mountain.*

White Bear I expect you're weary by now, Mari, so long and so far that you fared last night.

Mari I am not weary.

White Bear But you've been afraid, I imagine.

Mari Not afraid, either.

White Bear Don't you yearn to go home to your mother and father and all your siblings?

Mari You have said you shall do well by them all. I couldn't help them much back home in our cabin in the valley.

White Bear Are you not dissatisfied with our agreement, then?

Mari Oh no indeed! Look how the daylight gilds everything - how beautiful the highest peak grows over there.

White Bear Yes, it is soon time I went inside. Have you ever sat softer, have you ever seen clearer?

Mari No, never have I sat softer, and never have I seen clearer!

White Bear Yes, you are the right one! Hold on tight to my coat now, for here shall we descend.
(*They disappear, come down a slope along a shelf in the mountain, and stop before the door in the rock wall.*)

White Bear Now, Mari, we are here.
(*He knocks on the door in the mountain; it opens. We look into a magnificent hall.*)

White Bear Welcome to White Bear King Valemon's dwelling.
(*They enter the mountain; the door closes behind them.*)

Act II

Scene II - 1

In the white bear's parlour in the mountain.

In the foreground, stage left is a door. In the background, stage left, a corner fireplace where a fire burns. Stage right in the background is an alcove with a four-poster bed. Further down stage right is a long table with tablecloth and lighted candles.

Mari sits before the fireplace, spinning on a golden spinning wheel. She is dressed in a glossy silk gown of medieval cut, and has a crown on her head.

MARI Oh goodness, will night not soon fall? Time passes so slowly here, never with another living person to meet. If only I could understand why I should never see him. He is always so kind and good; he speaks so well and gently. When I stroke his face in the dark, I think he must be the most handsome man in the world, and I long to see my husband - just a little, mind. I suppose it's for the best, since he says it must be so. I suppose he does everything for my benefit; I understand that much. But goodness, how long the days are when one is always alone here in the mountain. Huff, I wish it soon were night.

WHITE BEAR (*without*) Open up! Open up for White Bear King Valemon!

> *The door swings open by itself; the* WHITE BEAR *enters.*

Are you sitting up even now, Mari - and in the dark here? I would have thought you'd have gone to bed a long time ago.

MARI I cannot sleep anyway.

WHITE BEAR You poor thing, are you downcast again, then?

MARI You should have some food now - I haven't eaten yet either, I get so tired of always sitting, eating alone.

> *She rings a small silver bell. The candles on the table light. Silver platters, wine jugs and goblets come hovering down from the ceiling and sit on the table.*

WHITE BEAR Then come here, my Mari, and sit next to me. Look here, drink some of this wine, and your heart will grow lighter.

> *They sit at the table.*

WHITE BEAR You mustn't grieve like this. I've said you must be patient. If only you are patient, then all will be well in the end. We shall move away from this mountain here, you shall see the sun and the moon and folk and land again, and you'll feel so much better than you can imagine. If only you can be patient - and then, you mustn't ask for anything.

MARI No, no, I won't ask. I will be patient enough. But now I wish I knew how things stood with my parents and siblings, at least.

WHITE BEAR They are just fine. And, oh yes - Kari, your middle sister is holding a wedding today with Tor Tofte.

MARI Goodness! What are you saying - Tor Tofte? He is the richest and handsomest boy in the great village. Indeed, shall Kari be the wife at Tofte and have Tor? I expect father and mother are happy!

WHITE BEAR Yes, they are. And they can thank you for it.

MARI Well, well. Oh, I wish I could see father and mother now - and Kari, my sister.

WHITE BEAR Perhaps you could see them. But only if I can be sure that you will do as I say and not forget it, but obey me. Then perhaps I could carry you home to your parents tomorrow. But you have to do as I say.

MARI I certainly will, you can depend on me.

WHITE BEAR You must try to say as little as you can about how things are here. They will fret and ask - be that as it may now. You may speak freely with your father and sisters. But don't speak alone to your mother about it - you have to promise me - and if she wants you to do anything other than what your father advises you, then don't listen to her, or you'll make us both unhappy.

MARI I shall certainly do as you desire.

WHITE BEAR Well, don't forget it. And now come, and we shall go to bed. The way is long to your father's farm, you know, so we must have a good rest before we go.

MARI Oh goodness, shall I really go home again, and see father and mother and Guri and Kari and all the children again - and go to Kari's wedding with Tor Tofte?

WHITE BEAR I would hate to deny you anything, my Mari - but keep in mind all that I have told you, now, lest you squander the happiness of both of us.

MARI I will be careful not to forget anything, King Valemon.

WHITE BEAR But let us go now to bed.
(The candles in the candleabras and the fire in the hearth are suddenly extinguished, and the stage is plunged into darkness.)

Scene II - II

The courtyard of a great farm.

Two white-painted main buildings in empire style. Log-built outbuildings, some painted red, others yellow-brown. Stage left in the foreground is a stretch of white-painted picket fence into the garden and a gazebo in empire style, with columns and doors facing outwards towards the audience.

The courtyard is full of wedding guests. Some are dressed as peasants, some as of a better class, others in city clothes from the 1820s.

Mari's mother (wearing a lace bonnet and dark checked silk dress) sits in the gazebo with the Provost's Wife *and some peasant wives,* Guri *(in a bonnet and shawl),* Kari *(a peasant's kirtle and a lace bonnet).*

They talk, knit and drink coffee. In the background, Ola *and the* Provost *walk up and down.[2] In the middle of the stage some young people are dancing. The master of the kitchen (with a staff decorated with flowers), and the*

---

[2] An ecclesiastical provost is a clergyman who holds a rank between the bishop and the parish priest.

master of the cellar (with a beer keg) walk around the courtyard and on the steps of the stabbur *storehouse.*[3]

THE DANCERS (*singing*)

> Here come the officers marching forth,
> with feathers in their hats and epaulettes.
> They offer the parson ten dollars, maybe twelve,
> They pass by the sexton and the floor does quelve.
> Oh humanity!
>
> Here come the soldiers marching forth,
> With belts round their middle and epaulettes
> They offer the parson five shillings on the hoof,
> They pass by the sexton, and offer their reproof.
> Oh humanity!
>
> Here come the citizens marching forth,
> With big woollen mittens, a staff in their hands,
> They offer the parson a shilling, maybe twain,

---

[3] A *stabbur* is a traditional log-built storehouse, used for storing foodstuffs such as bread, cured meats and dairy products.

They pass by the sexton, to the north they crane.
Oh humanity!
Here come the wives a-shuffling forth,
A drip from their noses and a single tooth,
They offer the parson according as they can,
They pass by the sexton, then they pass by their man.
Oh humanity!
Here come the girls stepping forth,
With bows at their neck and kerchiefs in their hands.
They offer the parson of what they can afford,
They pass by the sexton, and their finery he saw.
Oh humanity!
Oh look at the man by the cupboard there,
And look at all the money he gets so fair.
And look how everybody goes over for to see.
Oh shame on you; you must think of me.
Oh humanity!

The WHITE BEAR *and* MARI *enter between the outhouses, stage right, and stop behind a wall.*

MARI (*wearing a kirtle, but without a crown*) Oh no, oh no! Look at father and mother, look at sister and brother. Oh no, oh no! What a beautiful farm. Goodness, look at father - if he doesn't walk with the Provost, smoking a long pipe!

WHITE BEAR Are you happy then, Mari, now that you are at home again with your folks?

MARI Uff, it is so strange and unfamiliar that I am just confounded; wait a bit. I am just afraid to go and greet all these folk, I am.
(OLA *and the* PROVOST *in conversation, approach.*)

OLA ...well, no, the parson won't get me to sow these blessed potatoes next year. The apples were late to harvest, and they were small, and they didn't ripen, even though we let them sit on the straw for as long as we dared before the frost - and they remained just as green as they were when we picked them - and they were so bitter that they were completely inedible, said Marte-Marja, - I didn't even dare taste the stewed apples.

PROVOST Ha, ha, you've got it wrong, my good Ola. I understand you harvested the little green fruits that emerge after flowering - my good man, you have completely misunderstood. Beneath the earth, my friend - you should have sought the fruits of your labour beneath the earth. Just like a widower, the potato has its better part beneath the earth.

OLA The devil, you say! - excuse me - so it's a kind of turnip, then, this potato?

PROVOST No, by no means - however, it is high time I should seek out my better half - Christiane - we must take our leave of this pleasant company. As I said, my brave Ola, I shall in the near future, for the farmers, present in a dissertation what the common man should be made acquainted with regarding the cultivation of the potato. - Meanwhile, your ignorance in this area is wholly forgiveable, my good Ola, and will in no way detract from your agricultural merits, of which I intend to report to our newly formed Guild of Landholders.

(MARI *'s mother and the* PROVOST*'s* WIFE *come from the gazebo.*)

PROVOST'S WIFE Yes, you certainly have a lot to be grateful for, Marte-Marje - all three of your eldest daughters are married and live in good circumstances. It's just so unfortunate that your pretty little Mari couldn't come home for her sister's wedding - do I remember correctly that she wasn't home when Guri married Lieutenant Møller, either? Where do Mari and her husband actually live?

MARTE-MARJE Oh it is far from here - to the north.

PROVOST'S WIFE The north - indeed. Well, it must be a great loss for you, Marte-Marje. But the main thing is that you know that she's in good circumstances. And that she is, as far as I understand?

MARTE-MARJE Yes, she is (*weeps*)

PROVOST'S WIFE There, there, Marte-Marje. (*Pats her*)

> *The Provosts bid farewell.* MARTE-MARJE *goes back to the gazebo, with the corners of her apron before her eyes.*

MARI (runs forth, shouting) Mother, mother!

WHITE BEAR Do not forget what I have said to you. In three days, I shall come and fetch you.

> *Hurries out.*

MARI Good day, mother; good day, father.

EVERYONE Oh - oh - it's our Mari - Where have you come from? - Oh, how beautiful our Mari has grown! Welcome home, Mari.

> MARTE-MARJE *and* MARI *remain standing, hand in hand.*

MARTE-MARJE Oh, my dear child, have you really come home to us again?

MARI Oh mother, mother, how fine you have grown - and so beautiful. And such a lovely farm you have now. Oh father - have you got a pipe with silver lid too? - I'm so happy to be back at home that I could both jump and dance!

MARTE-MARJE Well, thank goodness we have you back home, Mari. Now, I expect you will be staying here for a good long while, won't you?

MARI I'm afraid I can't, mother. The White Bear King Valemon is coming to fetch me on the third day.

MARTE-MARJE You've been gone for three years, and we've neither heard nor asked of you - I say he might now have afforded our having you a little longer. But come into the gazebo for now, and have yourself a drop of coffee, while they make things ready inside - then you shall have dinner in a little while.

> *They go into the gazebo and sit down. The maid comes with fresh coffee and plates of cakes.*

MARTE-MARJE Imagine your coming back, Mari! I really can't look at you for long enough! Have you seen the like, as beautiful as your sister has grown, Guri and Kari?

GURI AND KARI No, it's true to say. And you look so foreign, too - I suppose you've come from afar? But now you must look across to Hov, and Tofte as well, and see how we fare.

MARTE-MARJE Yes, and greet Guri's husband - it's a real shame that our son-in-law the lieutenant had to leave early today - he is such a fine fellow, you see, and so handsome and genteel and kind, too.

OLA Oh, I expect Mari is used to fine folk by now.

GURI AND KARI Yes, tell us - let us hear some more about the kind of folk it is you live with, where you live. Is it a castle you live in?

MARI They call it such.

MARTE-MARJE But now you shall really have to be satisfied - no, would you look at that, the maid has forgotten to put out more candied sugar - Well, when we were up in the other place, I didn't at all consider that it might be a struggle to keep the servants in order, just making sure each does what he's supposed to. Yes, I'm sure you too know well, Mari; you probably have even more servants in your home than there are on the farm here?

MARI No, I have an easy time of it. I have a small silver bell, and when I ring it, everything that is needed is done. The table is covered and the floor is swept, and the bed makes itself, I think.

MARTE-MARJE Well, well, have you ever heard the like? Huff, no, I think that would be tedious in the long run. Isn't it a bit quiet for you when you don't have visitors?

MARI No visitors come where I live, mother.

MARTE-MARJE But dearest, don't you ever see anyone but your husband that way? Won't it be unbearable for you in the long run?

MARI No, I see none other than the White Bear. Sometimes it does get a little unbearable.

MARTE-MARJE He must be a transformed prince then, this bear of yours? What do you think?

MARI Yes, I think he is. Even though he has never said anything about it.

MARTE-MARJE But you can see it on him, if he is a prince?

MARI He never transforms himself before it is as dark as charcoal. I always have to put out all the lights before he comes to bed.

MARTE-MARJE But Jesus' cross! How can you tell what he looks like?

MARI I've never seen him at all, mother! (*weeps*)

MARTE-MARJE But, my God, my child, you can't tell if he's folk or troll!

GURI AND KARI Goodness, no, I couldn't bear to be married after that manner.

MARI Oh, he's not a troll - I love him so; he's so kind.

MARTE-MARJE You cannot know that if you've never seen him. You must see to it that you get to look upon him; you cannot be married to someone you've never seen!

MARI I'll have to endure it, I shall, mother, for he has said I must, and he is firm about it, too - that I must never try to look upon him before his time comes.

MARTE-MARJE But such is simply impossible. You have to come up with something, so you can catch a glimpse of him anyway -

OLA Now now, mother. Don't fool Mari into the wrong course. The White Bear's actions have been forthright and honorable, both with the girl and with all of us, I say; I expect he understands how he has to arrange things, both for himself and for others -

MARTE-MARJE Oh yes, it is easy for you to talk - it was you who wanted him to have Mari. Go up now, Guri and Kari, and see how our guests fare. Yes, you too, Ola.

OLA Thank you, but I am comfortable here.
(*Exit* GURI *and* KARI.)

MARTE-MARJE Sit down here with me, you my child, and we'll

talk a little, for we must find a way by which you can look upon this husband you are married to.

OLA No, no, woman; don't you fool Mari into disobeying her husband - it will only lead to misery, and not to happiness.

MARTE-MARJE Be quiet, Ola; you don't understand this! (*Shields her eyes from the sun with her hand.*)

MARTE-MARJE I say, is that not the Provost, trudging up the slope there? I wonder what he has turned around for. Hurry, Ola, run and meet him -

OLA Don't lure the girl into doing something she'll regret; I mean it! (*exit*)

MARTE-MARJE Look here, take this candle stub and hide it in your bosom, and these matches. - One night, when King Valemon is asleep, you can light the candle, just enough so that you may have a tiny glimpse of him. Just to see that he's a human.

OLA (*returning*) The Provost, you say - I saw no life down in the field other than your red calves. You shouldn't listen to your mother, Mari - she has always been so inventive.

MARTE-MARJE (*as they rise and walk up towards the buildings*) Do as I say, Mari; it's best for you!

Scene ii - iii

The hall in the mountain.

Enter White Bear *and* Mari.

White Bear Well, now you're back home again, Mari. I don't suppose you're quite so sullen, now that you have seen your folks?

Mari Oh, I'm not so sure. When I saw Guri and this lieutenant of hers, and Kari and Tor, then I was sad that I should never see you, my husband -

White Bear I hope you have remembered what I said you should do - you should listen to your father and not your mother, you know.

Mari You know I have remembered what you said to me.

White Bear That is well, then. But now I want to go to bed.

All the lights go out. After a while, Mari speaks in the darkness.

Mari No, I can't stand it anymore. I'll do it now - light mother's candle. I must be allowed a single glimpse, to see what he looks like, the man I have been given.

(Standing before the bed, Mari lights the candle. She is wearing a foot-length white nightgown, with her hair hanging loose over her shoulders. She lets the light fall upon King Valemon, who lies asleep in bed.)

MARI Oh! Oh! Oh! Can it be true that such a handsome man exists in the world? Oh, my husband, my husband - King Valemon, my dearest sweetheart!

She bends over him.

KING VALEMON (*awakens*) What is it? What was it that dripped on my chest and burned so? - Oh, Mari, Mari, what have you done? Now you have made us both unhappy!

MARI White Bear King Valemon - don't be angry with me!

KING VALEMON If only you had held out till the end of this year, I would have been saved. For I have a stepmother, who has bewitched me so that I am a white bear by day and a man by night. Now it's over between us, for now I must journey from you to her. She lives in a castle that lies East of the Sun and West of the Moon, and there too lives a princess with a nose three ells long, and she now shall I have.[4]

MARI (*on her knees*) Oh, White Bear King Valemon, White Bear King Valemon, don't leave me! -

---

[4] An ell is an old measure of about 45cm long.

KING VALEMON There is now nothing I can do about it, Mari - I must leave you.

MARI Can I not go with you, though?

KING VALEMON No, that is impossible.

MARI Can you not tell me the way, then, and I'll search for you - may I be allowed that?

KING VALEMON You may certainly be allowed. But no road goes thither. The castle lies East of the Sun and West of the Moon, and the way you will find late, perhaps never.

> *Thunder. It goes dark again. The light returns to reveal* MARI *lying on a small green knoll in the woods, weeping. What she had with her from home is beside her on the grass. It is early morning.*

MARI East of the Sun and West of the Moon, and the way you will find late, perhaps never. Even so, I shall now find you and win you, King Valemon, my friend. I shall wander and search - wander and search until I find you.

Act III

Scene III - I

Somewhere in the forest on the edge of a large marsh. Beneath an overhanging rock, between tall bearded spruces stands a ramshackle cabin. Outside sits an old woman.

MARI (*enters*) Good evening, mother.

FIRST OLD WOMAN Indeed. Now, nobody has called me mother for three hundred years. So I shall see if I can do you a proper motherly turn in return. You look as if you are both tired and hungry; sit down and rest, girl, and I'll go in and see if I can find you some food.

MARI Thank you; it's a shame you should take the trouble. But even so, I have so little time. I am looking for the prince, White Bear King Valemon, who is with his stepmother at the castle that lies East of the Sun and West of the Moon, and she wants to marry him to a princess who has a nose three ells long.

First Old Woman Do you know him, then? You must be the girl who should have had him; are you?

Mari Yes, that's me.

First Old Woman So that was you. Well, true to say, I don't know much more about him either. Yes, I have seen him, you know - when he journeyed and swept by here in the form of a bear. But otherwise I just know that he is said to live in a castle that lies East of the Sun and West of the Moon, and the way you will find late, perhaps never. But now I can do so much for you that I shall lend you my horse; he can carry you to the neighbouring wife - who is my sister, you see. Perhaps she may know the way. (*Calls*) Foola, foola, foola da!⁵

A saddled chestnut horse comes forth from the forest.

Now I shall go inside and put some food in your bag, and you can rest for a while in the meantime.

Enter a Mound Fellow *and a* Mound Hag. *They are old and overgrown with long, grey lichen, and have knapsacks on their backs.*

Both Good evening, good evening, my beautiful maiden.

---

⁵This call, and that in the next scene, is voiced in the manner of the traditional Norwegian *lokk*.

MARI (*rises and bobs*) Good evening, and thank you for last time.

THE MOUND FOLK Oh, you wouldn't happen to have a shilling or a bite of food to give to two poor old unfortunates?

MARI I'm afraid not. I have nothing but what I stand and walk in. I am out looking for the way to the castle that lies East of the Sun and West of the Moon, where White Bear King Valemon lives - I am trying to get there before his wedding to the troll daughter whose nose is three ells long.

THE MOUND FOLK Well, you don't need to rush, then, for he had a wedding with her last year. -

FIRST OLD WOMAN (*Enters with a packet of food*) What are you doing here, you rascals? Huff, they lie and they steal worse than folk. And then they go around sneaking and swiping, for they don't have so much as a mount to live in - not one of the mountain folk wants to give them shelter in their fields.

MARI Poor things - I pity the crooked old unfortunates. (*Takes off her black jacket and gives it to the* MOUND HAG.) Look here, take this; you need it more than I do.

MOUND HAG I only said it in jest - but you will have to hurry, girl, if you want to arrive before his wedding day. For we heard it from the crow, and she heard it from the eagle, and the eagle heard it from the cormorant, and she heard it from a bird far away from another country, that now they are slaughtering and brewing for a banquet at the castle that lies East of the Sun and West of the Moon.

They exit, running.

MARI I'm not certain I'll make it in time -

FIRST OLD WOMAN Don't worry about what those two nincompoops say! Even so, you shall have a quick ride. When you reach my sister, just strike the horse beneath its left ear and bid him go home again. And you can have this golden apple, too; it may be of some use, sometime -

MARI (*bobs*) Many thanks!

FIRST OLD WOMAN And see to it now that you come away. (*She hold the horse.* MARI *mounts and rides away.*)

Scene III - II

Mountain plateau with small tarns. The Ronde mountains lie far away in the distance.

In the foreground, beneath an overhanging slab sits the Second Old Woman, *winding balls of wool from a golden yarn swift.*[6]

Mari (*enter riding*) Good evening, grandmother.

Second Old Woman Good evening, good evening, indeed. Now, no one has called me grandmother. Well, not in six hundred years. So I think I shall try to do you a grandmotherly turn in return, I shall. You have come from my sister, I can see.

Mari Yes, I should greet you so diligently from her. She did so well that she lent me a horse. - She thought you might be able to tell me the way to the prince, White Bear King Valemon, who is with his stepmother at the castle that lies East of Sun and West of Moon.

Second Old Woman You know, I've seen him, of course - the time he went by here, he was in his bear form. But he

---

[6]A yarn swift is a rotor-like device that holds skeins of yarn in a manner that allows the yarn to be wound into balls without tangling.

hasn't come this way for a while, now, I don't think. - But what was it the hulder was saying about him a while ago?[7] I think she said there was a girl he should have - but that he'll now have to take a king's daughter who has a nose that is three ells long. I don't suppose you are this girl?

MARI Yes, that's me, sure enough.

SECOND OLD WOMAN Well, he lives East of the Sun and West of the Moon, he does, but more than that I don't know - and you'll find it late, perhaps never. But you could at least ask - the hulder may know more about it.

> *The* SECOND OLD WOMAN *calls. Enter a* HULDER. *She is very unkempt, her hair hangs loose and unbrushed, her skirt is in rags.*

Well, now you should hear something funny. Do you see this girl here? She comes from my sister. She is the one who should have had this prince - you know, the one we were talking about - White Bear King Valemon. And now she wants to see if she can find him again, she says -

HULDER (*laughs*) You're leaving it to the very last minute then,

---

[7] The hulder-folk is a hidden folk of Norwegian folklore. The cow-tailed female hulder is often portrayed as a temptress to good Christian menfolk.

girl - it's been three nights since the company travelled north; they cried that they were going to a banquet at the castle that lies East of Sun and West of Moon.

Mari These were tidings - if they aren't good, then you won't have told me for nothing. Look here, I have nothing to give you but my outer skirt. (*She slips out of it*)

Hulder (*angrily*) Are you going to snag me for my tail? (*She holds up her cow tail with one hand, takes the skirt in the other and exits, running.*)

Second Old Woman Never you mind her - the poor girl; she's been half silly since she went to the dance at the pasture at Samsal, when Nils the dragoon shot in over the heads of the party.[8] But now let me see if I can help you a little. (*Calling*) Foola, foola, foola da!

Enter a white horse, regally saddled.

You can borrow my horse, I think, and ride to my nearest neighbour; maybe she knows. Just strike the horse beneath its left ear and turn him back towards home when you arrive, and he will go straight home. And I want to give you this golden yarn swift - though I doubt

---

[8] Shooting over the heads of subterraneans is said to break all their enchantments.

you will need it. Now come on inside and get yourself a bite to eat before you move on.

Scene III - III

The basin of a fjord, surrounded by jagged, black mountains that plunge steeply toward a frozen lake on the valley floor. Ice fields and glaciers hang down over the rocks. In a hanging valley below a moraine sits the Third Old Woman, *spinning on a golden spinning wheel.*

Mari (*Enter riding, stops outside*) Good evening, good mother!

Third Old Woman Good evening, good evening, my child. Now, no one has called me good mother in nine hundred years. I shall have to do a good-motherly turn for you in return, I shall. What manner of beautiful girl are you, then? I see it is my sister who has sent you hither to me.

Mari Yes, I should greet you so diligently from your sisters. They sent me to you, for they thought that you might be able to tell me the way to the castle that lies East of the Sun and West of the Moon.

Third Old Woman Well, I know no more about it than that there is supposed be a prince whose stepmother wants him to marry a princess with a nose three ells long. There was another girl he should have had before - I don't suppose that is you?

Mari Yes it is, I'm afraid.

Third Old Woman Well, the castle certainly lies East of the Sun and West of the Moon, it does, but you will find it late, perhaps never. I don't know the way - but my brother's sons may know it. (My brother has four sons, you know, and they are called the East Wind and the West Wind and the South Wind and the North Wind.) If only I knew where to meet them … but that's it, you see - these fellows are not easy to get hold of - they are said to fare wide and blow strongly both early and late, so it is not so easy to meet them at home. But there I see the moon coming.

The Moon *rises over the ridge of the mountain.*

Hey there, Moon! You shine over all the world, and see far and wide - do you know where my brother's sons are blowing tonight?

Moon This night should all four rest. They whispered that they would meet here on the mountain tonight and play on the lake outside your cabin.

Third Old Woman Well, now you are lucky, my girl. If they do not know the way to this castle, then there is no one who knows it. Now I shall go inside and make you some food - and look here, take this golden spinning wheel - I think that perhaps you might need it. (*The* THIRD OLD WOMAN *goes in.*)

> *Enter the* EAST WIND, *the* WEST WIND *and the* SOUTH WIND, *soughing on great speckled wings. They begin to dance on the ice.*

MARI (*approaches*) Good evening, East Wind, good evening, West Wind, good evening, South Wind, can you tell me the way to the castle that lies East of the Sun and West of the Moon, - to White Bear King Valemon?

EAST WIND No, I certainly don't know the way, for I have never blown so far. But perhaps the West Wind knows it, for he is much stronger than I am.

WEST WIND No, I certainly don't know the way, for I have never blown so far. But I have heard from my brother, the South Wind, about this prince, White Bear King Valemon. Do you know the way to the castle that lies East of the Sun and West of the Moon, brother South Wind?

SOUTH WIND I have never blown so far. But I have heard of White Bear King Valemon. He shall marry the princess at the castle that lies East of the Sun and West of the Moon; she has a nose that is three ells long. Here comes our brother, the North Wind - hey, brother North

Wind, do you know the way to East of the Sun and West of the Moon?

NORTH WIND (*enters soughing down from a cleft*) Are you the girl who should have had White Bear King Valemon?

MARI Yes, that's me. Do you know the way to him?

NORTH WIND I know where it is. I once blew an aspen leaf thither, but then I was so tired that I couldn't bear to blow for many days. But if it is so that you are determined to journey, and you are not afraid to go with me, then I shall take you upon my back, and see if I can blow you thither.

MARI No, I am not afraid. For I must go to White Bear King Valemon, and I want to go to him, if there is any way to get there - even if things go ill, I want at least to try.

NORTH WIND Well, we should rest here until it draws towards the morning, then, for we must have the day ahead of us, if we are to get there. We must journey across both mountain and sea.

Act IV

Scene IV - 1

A room in the troll's castle. Foreground, stage right a bed. Stage left a door to another room. On the back wall an open door to a gallery with stairs down to the courtyard.[9] Late-afternoon lighting.

NORTH WIND (*Enters flying with* MARI *on his back, puts her down by the gallery steps.*) Well, Mari, now you are in the castle that lies East of the Sun and West of the Moon. I wish you good luck, now, Mari - I've helped you as far as I can; now you must do the rest yourself.

MARI Then you have my thanks for the ride. God helps those who help themselves, the old folk say in a proverb. I shall trust in that.

The NORTH WIND *disappears.* MARI *remains*

---
[9] Before the widespread adoption of the corridor, larger Norwegian houses were furnished with external galleries that gave entrance to different rooms.

standing in the gallery. Outside in the courtyard, a sleuth of white bears is passing by.

MARI *(runs down)* My White Bear, my White Bear, White Bear King Valemon, is that you? Are you here?

The bears continue running. A TROLL MAID *enters in a hurry.*

TROLL MAID What manner of ragged woman are you, who frightens our queen's pigs?

MARI I have heard that White Bear King Valemon is to have a wedding here at the castle - I thought one of these might be the groom.

TROLL DAUGHTER *(enters. She has a nose that extends all the way to the ground, and gold bracelets on her nose)* What manner of ragged girl are you, and why do you want to talk to my bridegroom?

The TROLL DAUGHTER *and the* TROLL MAID *enter the cabin and start making up the bed.* MARI *follows in through the door*

MARI Oh, it was just something I should have asked White Bear King Valemon - - -

TROLL DAUGHTER My bridegroom has nothing to speak with you about - not that I know of. He doesn't go about in the form of a bear, either - by the way. Those were my mother's pigs you saw -

MARI It's just that I have walked around, buying a few things. And I had some beautiful little things that I thought King Valemon would perhaps buy as a gift for his young bride.

TROLL DAUGHTER I don't need to ask my bridegroom for gifts; I can buy them myself. What do you have to sell, then?

MARI Oh, I have this beautiful golden apple - (*takes it forth and plays with it*). It might be nice for the bride to have in her hand, to play with on her big day.

TROLL DAUGHTER What do you want for it?

MARI It's not for sale, neither for gold, nor for money.

TROLL DAUGHTER If it isn't for sale for gold nor money, then what do you want for it? You can have whatever you want for it.

MARI I want to come in here tonight and stay with the prince who lies here.

TROLL DAUGHTER Well, I think I must ask my mother if you can have that. Mother - mother!

TROLL QUEEN (*enters*) Yes, what is it, my beautiful doll?

TROLL DAUGHTER Mother, there is a ragged girl here who has a gold apple she wants to sell. But she says it's not for sale for gold or money. She wants to be allowed to come into White Bear King Valemon's chamber, and stay there tonight, she says -

TROLL QUEEN Well, if that will be fun for her, then ... (*laughs*). You can let the girl in after you have given King Valemon his evening drink you, my silk doll - can she enjoy herself watching him sleep; we may gladly let her have that.

TROLL DAUGHTER (*to* MARI) Yes, mother says, you may do it. And now you can let me have the golden apple. Now, out you go until I call you.

> *Exit* MARI. *The trolls follow. Immediately after, enter three small princesses in white dresses and golden crowns, wearing pantalettes, and silk scarves about their waists; then King Valemon, stage left.*

SMALL PRINCESSES Now you have sat up in the tower, scouting and watching all day, King Valemon - won't you ever come down and play with us again?

WHITE BEAR You poor things! If only you knew what it will mean, both for you and for me, that the one I am waiting for arrives on time -

SMALL PRINCESSES Have you seen nothing of the one you're waiting for?

WHITE BEAR No, even though I have been at the top of the tower all day. Or until that big gust of wind came, at least - then it grew so blustery and dusty that I could see nothing, and so I came down. But now you should go to bed, or else my stepmother the troll hag will come and beat you with her broom, you know.

SMALL PRINCESSES *(bob)* Good night, King Valemon. *(exit, running)*

WHITE BEAR Well, now there's not long left, either. Oh, you are here again, then!

Enter the TROLL DAUGHTER, *carrying a golden horn*[10]

Can I never have peace from you, Big Nose? We are going to have a wedding in three days - can't you be happy with that?

TROLL DAUGHTER Yes, I'm very happy. I'm just afraid you're going to fall ill before our wedding day, for you always stand up in the tower in the cold wind, and that's why I've brewed a drink for you, which will do you good.

WHITE BEAR Thank you; I'm not thirsty.

---

[10] A drinking horn, in the manner of the Vikings.

TROLL DAUGHTER Well, I won't leave until you've drunk it.

WHITE BEAR Indeed. You won't? Then let me have it.

> *The* TROLL DAUGHTER *gives King Valemon the horn, he empties it, then throws himself on the bed. Exit the* TROLL DAUGHTER, *then immediately enter* MARI.

MARI King Valemon - King Valemon - you who said that to the castle that lies East of the Sun and West of the Moon I would come late, perhaps never - do you see that I have come anyway?
King Valemon, King Valemon, wake up!
Wake up, King Valemon, it's Mari! - Oh, I have travelled far and farther than far, I have travelled over mountain and valley, I have ridden upon the back of the North Wind -
King Valemon, don't you hear? It's Mari. Mari! It's Mari! Oh, what should I do to waken him?
King Valemon, you're not dead, are you? Oh no, he's breathing. And I cannot awaken him.

> MARI *throws herself, weeping, across the bed.*

Scene IV - II

Same place. Mari *sits in the doorway, spinning on the golden spinning wheel. Enter the* Troll Queen *and the* Troll Daughter.

Troll Queen Good evening, my raggedy girl. Well, how do you think the trade is working for you?

Mari Well, thank you. I am soon sold out of everything I brought with me, both my golden apple and the golden yarn swift. It's a shame to complain.

Troll Queen And are you satisfied with your trade?

Mari Oh indeed. I am so satisfied that I could sell something more for the same price, I could.

Troll Queen What do you have to sell today, then?

Mari Well, now I have nothing but this golden spinning wheel - but you know, your daughter might well need it, now that she is getting married. Don't you want it, troll daughter?

Troll Daughter I do indeed. But don't you want something else for it this time?

Mari No, it is not for sale, neither for gold nor for money. The price is the same as on the other two occasions.

Troll Daughter Mother, are you sure this is a good idea? You know, my raggedy girl, I can give you as much as you want of gold and money - won't you rather have money for the spinning wheel?

Mari No, I set the price of my things in the manner that I want -

Troll Queen Don't worry about it, my dear. (*To* Mari) Yes, it is a good trade, my raggedy girl.

Take comfort, my beautiful child - my golden hen - tonight we will brew the drink so strong that King Valemon will not be fully awake from his stupor until he is wedded to you.

Now, off you go, my raggedy girl. We shall call you when you can come in to King Valemon.

Exit Mari

Troll Queen What are you standing there, moping about, my goat?

Troll Daughter Oh, I am so heavy of mind and sorrowful tonight, mother - I don't like this ragged girl doing her trade around here -

Troll Queen But you like the things she sells, don't you?

Troll Daughter Well I am also sorrowful and heavy-minded, for it's as if King Valemon doesn't hold me as dear as I hold King Valemon.

TROLL QUEEN Take comfort you, my daughter; you shall have him anyway. (*The* SMALL PRINCESSES *look in*) Out with you children! What are you flying about here, staring at?

TROLL DAUGHTER Oh, I'm so sorrowful and heavy-minded, I don't like your keeping these three ugly Christian-man's children around here either. It would be much better, I think, if you had them slaughtered, and roasted them for our wedding.

TROLL QUEEN Shut up! Don't just sit there, jawing. I told you: I promised the three princesses to my nephews, the three giants in the Grey Hills. You never think of anything but yourself. That's the thanks a mother has - here I've been around for a hundred years, striving and toiling and witching to keep you satisfied - out you go, you sorry ghost - out with you too, children. But go carefully down the stairs, now, my golden hen; it's so dark here - hold your nose up, there, my child, so you don't stumble over it.

Exit the SMALL PRINCESSES *to the gallery. The* TROLL QUEEN *and* TROLL DAUGHTER *follow.*

KING VALEMON (*enter stage left, carrying a lighted candle, which he puts down. He begins to undress.*) Well, now it's night again

- the last one. Now there is nothing more to wait for. Even so, the moon will rise in a little while. Perhaps I should go up the tower again - no, oh no, I know it's no use. No one can find the way hither. No, she will never find the way hither!

SMALL PRINCESSES (*look in*) King Valemon, King Valemon!

KING VALEMON Yes, what do you want with me? You poor things, there is no more hope that we will be delivered, neither you nor I. Tomorrow I have to marry the Big Nose. And then your turns will come; you are to have her mother's three brother's sons - they have three and six and nine heads.

SMALL PRINCESSES Listen to us, King Valemon. When the troll daughter comes to give you the sleeping draught this evening, pretend to drink it, but let the drink run out instead. A girl has been with you last night and the night before; she wanted to talk to you, but for all her crying and weeping and carrying on, she couldn't wake you.

KING VALEMON What are you saying?

SMALL PRINCESSES No, we dare not speak to you more - some of the trollfolk may notice it - and there comes Big Nose down in the courtyard. The girl said she is called Mari.

Exit, the SMALL PRINCESSES, *running. King Valemon throws himself on to the bed, and pulls the bedspread over himself. Enter the* TROLL DAUGHTER *with the golden horn.*

TROLL DAUGHTER Here's your evening drink, King Valemon.

KING VALEMON Yes, hurry up and bring it here, so I may be rid of your ugly face.

TROLL DAUGHTER Huh-huh-huh! Should you talk like that to your young bride on the evening before your wedding day?

KING VALEMON That's why I want peace from you until tomorrow. Go now. Goodness, I grow so sleepy from that drink - now I shall sleep (*snores*).

TROLL DAUGHTER King Valemon (*King Valemon snores*). King Valemon, here is one who wants to talk to you! (*King Valemon snores louder*) Hi-hi-hi! It will be some talk she'll have with him. Yes, now you can come in to the prince, my raggedy girl.

She lets MARI *in, blows out the candle so that the moonlight outside fills the stage, goes out and locks the door.*

MARI King Valemon. (*King Valemon snores as loudly as he can.*)

Mari (*weeping*) Oh, shall it be just the same - on this, the last night.

King Valemon (*whispers*) Oh, Mari, Mari, don't weep; make sure she doesn't stand skulking outside. (*He snores loudly*)

Mari (*approaches the door*) Oh, I'm so happy I hardly believe my own ears. No, no one is here - King Valemon, are you awake?

King Valemon (*jumps on to the floor*) Yes, my Mari, I am awake (*they fly into each other's arms*) - although I almost think I must be dreaming. Have you found your way hither, my true bride? Have you found your way to the castle that lies East of the Sun and West of the Moon?

Mari Yes, I have wandered both farther than far, and farther still. Had I not been able to ride with the North Wind at last, then I would have arrived late, perhaps never.

King Valemon Yes, you came at the last moment. I am supposed to marry long nose tomorrow.

Mari Then we must flee at once.

King Valemon It would be of little use if we tried to flee - we would never come so far that my stepmother could not reach us again with her trollish enchantments. But now that you are here, there is a piece of advice by which we may defeat the witch; but no one in the world can use it except you. I'll tell you now, and then you shall have to tell me all about your journeys.

Scene IV - III

The courtyard of the troll castle.

The cabin with the gallery in the background. Foreground, stage left a well. The courtyard is full of Troll-Wedding Guests. *Saddled bears, wolves, reindeer, troughs and tubs drawn by cockerels and toads.* Mari *in her rags sits by the well. The* Small Princesses *and some captured Christian-folk look down from the gallery.*

Troll Hag Lord Thurs! Will we not soon be ready to go?

Troll Queen (*enters from the outhouse, stage right*) You must excuse me, my dear Sigurrós, but I had to take a look at the food.[11] Can you imagine! The new cook had put worm suet in the wedding cake, and she used the toad vomit that I told her to whip and put on top of the cake to roast the badger in. she has boiled the cowbane to death in the viper soup. And she says she's finished her apprenticeship. She has served the fellow in the midden at Hedal for two hundred years, but she's no better than this!

Troll Hag Girls nowadays! There are almost none to be found but hulders - and they're almost as bad as folk -

---

[11]The significance of the proper names Thurs and Sigurrós escapes me.

and they want time off every blessed Thursday evening, and both twice and three times a week otherwise - flying out and about with the sons of Christians from the villages. Then they tarry, and sleep at home in the mountain ...

TROLL QUEEN Indeed, you said it. No, it's not been possible to get a real cookwife for a troll banquet since old mother gyger in Kjerringberget stopped going out. But here comes my daughter.

Enter TROLL DAUGHTER *in her bridal finery*

TROLL DAUGHTER Hey, hey hey - oh hey oh hey, for the bride!

They dance around her

But is my bridegroom not coming, King Valemon?

KING VALEMON (*in the gallery doorway*) Yes, here he is.

TROLL DAUGHTER But you are not dressed up for the wedding, King Valemon - are you going to ride to the troll church in your everyday clothes, then?

KING VALEMON (*angry*) Well, I shall have to - I don't have the shirt that I said I wanted as my bridegroom's shirt, and so the rest doesn't matter

TROLL HAG I laid out a silk shirt that was just as nice.

KING VALEMON But I said I wanted the linen shirt with the three tallow spots on it, and I will not stand as bridegroom in anything else. Hurry, my bride, let me see that you have the skill to wash it clean.

TROLL QUEEN It won't be dry; use your sense.

KING VALEMON Then I can wear it wet. I say this, and I swear it on my Christian-man's faith: I will not marry any other bride than she who can wash that shirt whiter than freshly fallen snow.

TROLL QUEEN Well, then you must try, my daughter - the shirt is in the bucket by the well.

> *The* TROLL-WEDDING GUESTS *go over to the well and crowd around the* TROLL DAUGHTER.

TROLL DAUGHTER (*wimpering*) Mother - I cannot get the tallow drops out of it. They run. The more I scrub and rub, the worse it grows.

TROLL QUEEN Oh, you clumsy thing - have you ever seen such a three-handed girl - come, let me ...

ONE OF THE SMALL PRINCESSES Now it looks as if it's lain in the ground.

THE HULDERS Come here with it, old mother - come, let us wash it - we want White Bear King Valemon - we will not let your daughter have him -

King Valemon *(calls)* How is it going, over there?

Small Princesses They fight and pull - it's strange that they haven't torn the shirt to ribbons by now.

King Valemon Oh, the shirt will survive for as long as the stains.

Small Princesses Well, they cannot remove the stains - now it looks as if the shirt has been pulled through the chimney.

King Valemon *(calls)* Come here with my shirt - let me see how you have managed!

> *The* Troll-Wedding Guests *come over with a charcoal-black shirt, which they pull between themselves.*

King Valemon Oh, you wash like a pack of trolls. I'm sure that ragged girl sitting over there could wash my shirt much better than all of you put together. Come here you, girl; will you see if you can wash my shirt white?

Mari You know, I can always try *(goes to the well)*

Small Princesses Oh look, look! As soon as she dipped it in the water.

Mari *(returns with a snow-white shirt)* Now the tallow drops are washed off, which spilled on your shirt, King Valemon, my bridegroom, that night in the mountain, when I disobeyed you and lighted upon you!

KING VALEMON And now you have loosed me from the enchantment!

> *Thunder and lightning. Darkness. When the light returns, the* TROLL-WEDDING GUESTS *have gone – the last balls of grey yarn roll off to the wings.*[12] *The mountain-stricken Christian-folk with the three little princesses at their head storm out from the gallery.*[13]

MOUNTAIN STRICKEN We are saved, we are free, we are loosed from the mountain.

KING VALEMON And here is she who has loosed us all. She is my true bride and I shall marry her and have her as my queen!

MOUNTAIN STRICKEN Hail, hail, hail, King Valemon and his bride. Hail King Valemon and Queen Mari!

---

[12] Balls of grey yarn are often associated with subterranean creatures, such as trolls and hulders, in Norwegian folklore.

[13] The mountain-stricken are the Christian-folk who have been abducted and held by the subterraneans.

About the Author

Sigrid Undset (1882-1949) is Norway's most successful female author of all time. Her literature broaches all manner of topics and themes, but she found her niche in historical fiction, winning the Nobel Prize in Literature in 1928 for her *Kristin Lavransdatter* trilogy (published 1920-1927).

Having taken a strong, outspoken stance against the policies of the Nazis during the 1930s, Undset was forced to flee when Norway was invaded in 1940. She found her way to the United States by way of the Soviet Union and Japan, and spent the rest of the war supporting the Allied war effort through her writing. She moved back to Norway in 1945, and died at home four years later.

About the Translator

Simon Roy Hughes has lived in Scandinavia since 1991, northern Norway since 1992. He is keen to see Norwegian folklore available in English translation, and to that end has published *Erotic Folktales from Norway* (2017), Peter Christen Asbjørnsen's version of *The Three Bears* (2019), as well as *Five Norwegian*  *White Bear Tales* (2019). He holds a *Cand. Philol.* degree from the University of Tromsø, and a PGCE from Bodø University College (now Nord University). By day he works as a lecturer in middle school.

Drafts of his translations are available to read online: http://norwegianfolktales.blogspot.com/

He is also on Twitter, as @SimonRoyHughes

Printed in Great Britain
by Amazon